In this series –

RUMI READINGS
FOR
CAREERS & WORK

RUMI READINGS
FOR
CAREERS & WORK

JALALUDDIN RUMI

The Scheherazade Foundation

The Scheherazade Foundation CIC
85 Great Portland Street
London
W1W 7LT
United Kingdom
www.SF.Charity
info@SF.Charity

First published by The Scheherazade Foundation CIC, 2025

RUMI READINGS FOR CAREERS & WORK

A CIP catalogue record for this title is available from the British Library.

ISBN 978-1-915311-69-6

Introduction

Jalaluddin Rumi was born in Balkh, Afghanistan, in the year 1207, and died in Konya, Turkey, in 1273.

During the sixty-six years spanning this pair of dates, he produced a range of extraordinary work in Persian which, today, is classed as 'Sufi Mysticism'.

In the seven and a half centuries since his death, Rumi's corpus, which includes *The Masnavi* and *Fihi Ma Fihi*, has been circulated widely across the Near East, the Arab world, and Central Asia.

Generations of students continue to commit selections of the 60,000 verses to heart, and allow Rumi's way of thought to permeate through all areas of their lives.

Although Orientalists venturing eastward from Europe in the 1700s occasionally made note of Sufi Mysticism, they tended to witness it through the more theatrical frills – such as 'whirling dervishes' – rather than through a deep appreciation of the texts.

It wasn't until the close of the nineteenth century that the first wholescale translations of Rumi's written work began to appear in Europe.

Even then, they remained very much the purview of a few academics, whose translations were – even for the time – laden with indescribably floral and cumbersome prose.

Although in the Occident, students would find themselves scrutinizing Rumi's corpus, it wasn't until more recently that accessible appreciations of his work became available.

A few years before his death, I asked my father – the Sufi scholar and thinker Idries Shah – for his thoughts on Rumi's legacy in the West.

Sitting in his favourite chair, a porcelain cup of green tea in hand, he looked at me hard.

'I never cease to be amazed,' he said.

'Amazed by what?'

'By the way people don't take what's perfectly packaged, and ready and waiting for them, but rather obsess with something else.'

'With what?'

'With endless and nonsensical trimmings, trappings, and paraphernalia.'

My father sipped his tea.

After a moment of silent thought, he continued:

'Read Rumi in the original Persian,' he said, 'and so delicate are the verses that you have tears rolling down your cheeks. Yet here in the West, it's served up as something submerged in a thick, glutinous gravy, so much so that its utterly inedible.'

I reminded my father that a series of publications had recently found their way to press – publications that presented Rumi's couplets in an utterly new way.

Stripped bare of what my father had referred to as 'gravy', they were light.

Indeed, they were lighter than light.

My father rolled his eyes at the thought.

'In any other place, and at any other time,' he said, 'people would be up in arms. Or, if they weren't, they'd be laughing until their sides split. Imagine it – Western poets with absolutely no knowledge of the original Persian text touting new, bestselling editions of Rumi's work! It's what we call "The Soup of the Soup of the Soup".'

In the years since my father's death, Occidental society has been flooded with all things Rumi.

Couplets ascribed to him are read solemnly at weddings across the United States, Europe, and beyond.

Wisdom drawn from his poetry is tattooed daily over the backs and limbs of Hollywood A-listers.

But the precious words uttered at weddings, tattooed into skin, and quoted in abundance, hold little or no bearing to the original verses of Jalaluddin Rumi.

So, there it is…

The great Sufi Master's wisdom available:

(a) in a form that's unreadable because it's all covered in glutinous gravy, or

(b) in another form that's completely distorted – the Soup of the Soup of the Soup.

One thing that *is* evident is that the West can benefit enormously from a clean, clear rendition of Rumi's thinking – as the East has done over the last seven hundred years.

For this reason, we have commissioned entirely new translations, gleaned in particular from *The Masnavi*. Selected and translated by native Persian-speaking scholars, the emphasis has been on maintaining the lightness of Rumi's poetry.

In an age of relentless speed and digital overload, and so as to allow the work to be accessed by those who may benefit from it most, we have arranged a series of bite-sized morsels by way of theme.

We encourage you to do what students, scholars, and ordinary people have done across the East for centuries...

To pick a single couplet, or a handful – and to read them over and over, allowing them to seed themselves in your mind.

Little by little, having taken root, they will blossom and bear fruit.

Tahir Shah

How to Use This Book

Rumi Readings for Careers & Work

This book is for everyone who works.

Whether you work with your hands, your heart, or your voice.

Whether your labour is celebrated or invisible.

Whether you're leading others or just trying to hold yourself together through the day.

It's for those who feel called to something more – and for those who feel trapped in something less.

Rumi Readings for Careers & Work brings the voice of a 13th-century mystic into the modern world of employment, ambition, purpose, burnout, and uncertainty. These verses were not written for CEOs or sages alone. They were written for anyone trying to live meaningfully – in the market, in the fields, at the desk, or behind the scenes.

Each quote has been freshly translated from the original Persian by scholars working with The Scheherazade

Foundation. They are presented in ten thematic parts – from the value of persistence and creativity, to questions of justice, true wealth, and the impact of our work on the soul.

This is not a manual. It is not a theory of success.

It is a companion.

Let these quotes sit beside you as you navigate your work – whatever shape that work takes today.

A Still Voice in a Noisy World

Work, in modern life, is often accompanied by noise – pressure, comparison, self-doubt, performance metrics, the churn of productivity. It's easy to forget the deeper meaning behind what we do.

This book offers you moments of stillness. Not to stop you from working – but to help you remember why it matters.

You don't have to read it all at once. You don't even have to 'understand' every line. Just open it when something in your day feels stuck, confusing, or in need of perspective.

Let the words find you.

One Quote at a Time

Try reading a single quote in the morning before your day begins. Or during a quiet break. Or as a ritual at the end of a long shift.

Read it aloud. Sit with it for a moment. Ask yourself:

- What is this reminding me of?
- What part of my work is asking for more presence?
- How do I bring meaning to what I do?

If you're keeping a journal, copy the quote down. Let it lead you into reflection.

You don't have to write long reflections. You don't have to reach conclusions. The act of *pausing* is itself a form of inner work.

A Guide for Change and Continuity

This book can meet you in times of transition – when you're considering a new path, leaving a job, starting over, or simply questioning the direction you're going. But it's also for the steady seasons, when you're showing up every day and wondering if it still matters.

Rumi's words remind us that external success is not the only measure. There is dignity in effort. There is wisdom in repetition. There is soul in even the smallest task – if we remember to look.

Read It With Others

You may find certain quotes resonate with colleagues, students, employees, or clients.

Consider sharing a passage at the start of a meeting. Or leaving one posted in a shared space.

You never know who might be needing it that day.

Rumi's voice is clear and universal. His words have long been used to bring people together – across cultures, across generations, across roles.

This Is Work, Too

Reading this book – and taking it seriously – *is* a kind of work. It is the work of realigning. Of reconnecting. Of returning to the core of why we do what we do.

It is not an escape from responsibility. It is an invitation to meet it with more depth.

Rumi writes: '*If you do not rise with determination, you remain at the level of dust. But with resolve, you can attain the pinnacle of excellence.*'

Let this book help you rise – not just in position, but in clarity, integrity, and meaning.

Whatever your work looks like today, let it become a path.

Not just to what you produce –but to who you are becoming.

Part 1
The Benefits of Diligence in Work

1

The bird uses its wings to fly to the nest;
O people,
your wings of are those of diligence!

2

If you are a prince,
hold your head high
and do not settle for a mere crown from the king.
Shed your robes and enter the water of life,
that rubies and gems may grow
from your broken pieces of earth.

3

Day and night,
the Universal Mind is driven mad with desire
when it detects even the slightest indication of lesser desire.
Because mind recognizes the inferiority of all other goals
in the face of its own aspiration.

4

Like crows surrounding the dead,
I do not circle back to collect living prey
when I return as a falcon.
Crow, come and turn yourself into a falcon.
Before the Pure One,
purify yourself of your crow-like nature.

5

Living in a house of sadness is a sign
of low determination.
How can someone with little resolve
allow secrets to live in their heart?
The heart of a lover is higher than the heavens,
so know that you are deserving of whatever
it is that makes you quiver.

6

Keep your resolve strong,
because if it is weak,
the king's envoy will turn you away.
Who will help you go forward?
Speak without words and in silence,
like the angels in the clear blue sky.

7

Keep your resolve strong,
because unwavering love draws
free spirits and chosen kings.
He is the sun, and we are the darkness and the earth.
He drives the night away with the sword
of a dawn full of day.

8

The chain-mover came to give thanks
to the good fortune of the sorrowful
and the persistence of the passionate;
may the wind blow thus!

9

If you do not rise with determination,
you remain at the level of dust.
But with resolve, you can attain the pinnacle of excellence.
You can fulfil the decrees of fate that have passed
by delving into the depths of contemplation.

10

A falcon, though pure and unmatched in its whiteness,
becomes insignificant
when its prey is nothing more than a mouse.

Part 2
Imitation or Creativity?

11

Imitation captures the heart with its imprint,
blinding eyes with tears like flowing water.
For imitation embodies a quiet virtue,
a steadfast monument towering like a mountain.

12

While your mind soars upward,
your bird of imitation pecks at the ground below.

13

It is lamentable that we sit here
claiming imitation as our own knowledge;
it restrains the wing of our spirit
even when employed,
asserting that what we know has intrinsic origin.

14

Do not be like sugar before parrots.
Rather, be like poison, safe from harm.

15

They cast me into the wind of their imitation.
May two hundred curses fall upon that imitation!

16

Followers often justify their actions
with numerous analogies,
rather than relying on factual evidence.
The substance they offer is contaminated,
not authentic, musk,
for while it may carry the scent of musk,
it is nothing but dirt.

17

The imitator faces considerable danger:
straying from the path,
preyed on by thieves,
influenced by Satan,
and falling under a curse.

18

Imitators are easily swayed by external influences,
lacking conviction.
Like a ship without an anchor,
they become vulnerable,
unable to navigate treacherous waters.

19

Driven by greed,
imitation distracts their mind
from enlightenment and brilliance.

20

When a thief enters a house,
he assumes the guise of someone who lives there.
But eventually it dawns on him
that the house he has entered is his own.

Part 3
The Role of Free Will in Accomplishing Tasks

21

In every endeavour you pursue,
your personal strength will shine through.

22

In this world,
we have the ability for independent choice and action,
which is undeniable,
based on our clear perception
through the senses.

23

Authority, constraint, anger, honour, and criticism
are unique to the person endowed with autonomy,
O virtuous individual!

24

Exercise your autonomy;
do not become fatalistic.
If you have strayed from the right path,
examine your actions and avoid further deviation.

25

Exerting control over the weak
is within the capability of everyone.
It is rare, however, for someone to submit
to His will with such
determination and obedience,
like a devoted servant.

26

Consciously strive to grasp and accept absolute reality.
Transform into a state devoid of selfish desires
and personal volition.
Then, the wine's fullness will bear stronger spirits,
and you will be fully forgiven,
like an intoxicated soul.
The wine echoes your every word,
guiding your every step.

27

Choice is a boon for those
who are determined
in their commitment to their principles.
In the absence of safeguards and devotion,
beware of the Devil and reject tempting options.

28

You have consciously chosen a profession.
You possess both the skill
and the ability for deep contemplation.
Once you have chosen that occupation,
O Lord,
when the time arrives for life and breath,
twenty deceased souls will come to you
from all areas of life.

29

Autonomy is an essential aspect of worship,
like salt for food.
Without it, the celestial sphere would not rotate.
Its turning is beyond praise or criticism.
Autonomy promotes the practice of accountability.

30

Humans, blessed with intelligence and spirit,
have the power to overcome mountain, sea, and abyss.

Part 4

Performing or
Not Performing a Task

31

When greed blocks the sun,
it would be strange
for it to illuminate the path.

32

He proclaimed,
'I am a devoted servant of God,
hailing from His divine garden.
When I eat dates from the tree,
it is a gift bestowed upon me by Him.'
O people,
Why do you throw accusation against him?
The meal given him is meagre.
He immediately fastened it to the tree,
and then struck his back and leg hard with a stick.
He is a devout follower of God,
serving Him faithfully,
yet he strikes another servant on his back.

33

'Compulsion' restrains affection,
while those devoid of love
find themselves trapped by compulsion.
This intimacy is a genuine connection with Truth,
not something imposed or artificial.
It is the embodiment of beauty,
not something obscured or hidden like clouds.

34

From this viewpoint,
the act of bowing down intensifies desire;
not taking action dispels feelings of obligation and lethargy.
Compulsion serves as the driving force behind perfection,
but it may also act as confinement
and enslavement for those who lack motivation.

35

In the face of the power of creation,
every being is impotent,
like ants in the presence of a needle.
At times, this power assumes the appearance of the devil,
at others, that of Adam,
switching between happiness and sorrow.

36

We all possess the qualities of lions,
but the lion of knowledge is greatest.
Its attack is swift and unpredictable,
coming on the wind, moment by moment.

37

Prophets are driven
by their involvement in earthly concerns,
while disbelievers are driven
by their involvement in matters of the afterlife.
The prophets prioritize matters of the hereafter,
while the ignorant prioritize matters of the world.

38

You did not ascribe weakness to the Truth.
Rather, you labelled the uneducated
as perplexed and ignorant.

39

If the state of the world is not solely determined by destiny,
why do events unfold in opposition to happiness?
Fate governs both positive and negative outcomes,
as all plans are liable to mistakes.

40

I have been ensnared by the scheming of tyrants,
my physical strength drained by their use of force.
Henceforth, I will disregard their whisperings,
as their words are like evil spirits.

Part 5

Examining the Drawbacks of Power in Conducting Affairs

41

Making themselves unhappy
to escape anonymity,
people overlook the manacle of fame and reputation.
How is this any less constraining than iron itself?

42

Selling your attractiveness
can lead to misfortune.
Envy drives enemies ruthlessly to separate them,
while even friends will gradually exploit them.

43

The craving for fame
is like an animal's need for food.
When pursuing power,
this longing only intensifies.

44

Many can partake in a communal meal,
but an ambitious person cannot share
the world with others.

45

He feels intense pain
on discovering something,
and completely destroys it.
If he finds nothing,
he destroys himself.

46

In our times
this truth is undeniable:
you are enslaved by material possessions.
The one who seeks to possess and control
is perilously close to their own downfall.
From an upside-down viewpoint,
confined within this realm,
you have bestowed
upon yourself the title of ruler of this dominion.

47

They proudly claim to possess divine authority.
But can anyone who seeks companionship
be excluded?

48

If someone attempts to impress you,
respond with a rebuke:
direct financial resources and assets go towards those
who are impoverished and in need.

49

Some have placed their trust
in fraudsters and charlatans,
relying on illusory security:
a dome made of bubbles.
In the end, that 'tent' is nothing more
than a length of rope.

50

The kings of the world,
because of their excessive indulgence,
were unable to perceive the essence
of profound devotion.

Part 6
The Intersection of Justice & Injustice in Actions

51

When a person falls into a pit
that they have dug themselves,
it is their own actions
that caused the outcome.
The darkness of the well deepens
with the deeds of the unjust.
The wise and the knowing understand this:
the greater the injustice,
the deeper and more terrifying the abyss becomes,
as justice determines that
the unworthy must endure even greater misfortune.

52

A mosquito ventured forth from the garden,
seeking sustenance from plants.
Solomon transformed the insect
into a symbol of justice and equity.
'Solomon, through your dispensation of justice,
you exercise authority over jinns, humans, and fairies.'

53

The evil ruler
who once brought death to the entire planet,
has now been resurrected,
and every individual
has become a follower of God.
Abandon your own self-importance;
restore the world;
destroy the tyrant;
subject them to servitude.

54

Evil practices originating
from the first king now
continue with each successive action.
Anyone who practises unpleasantness
will face an unending stream of curses.
While the virtuous depart,
these customs endure,
and oppression and malediction
persist from the wicked.

55

Guides repeatedly caution against overstepping
boundaries, acting as brakes for the hurtling chariot.
Such actions tarnish reputations,
sow disharmony, and breed discontent,
traits characteristic of those
who propagate corruption in society.

56

The Prophet once said,
'It is better to face animosity caused by ignorance
than to show compassion to a fool.'
This wisdom underlines a stark truth:
despots see hearts as charred meat from their own fires.
May you find the strength to stand firm
against all enemies.

57

The throne trembles
under the burden of praise for the wicked
masquerading as accolades for the virtuous.

58

When a judge accepts a bribe,
distinguishing between perpetrator
and victim becomes impossible.
Numerous blameless adherents perish,
seeking solace in the faith of Moses
and the past.

59

The courageous are invaluable to society.
When the cries of the downtrodden echo out,
the brave are recognized as expressions
of divine benevolence.

60

Have you ever witnessed
a fleeting moment ascend to the heavens?
Sadly, such an event has never occurred.
Yet, if you remain vigilant and attentive,
you will discern the immediate consequences
of your actions in every instance.

Part 7

Examining the Relationship Between Cause & Effect

61

Actions exhibit a chain-like nature,
where each cause surpasses its corresponding result.
Stone and iron outperform mere sparks.

62

He obviates the perpetuation of those causes,
and the means to actualize them remain unknown.
Indeed, the true originator of outcomes is He,
but those who focus on superficiality
fail to perceive anything beyond
the immediate cause.

63

The absence of the fundamental reason
ultimately leads to deprivation,
as the compound of effort towards the cause dissipates.
How can someone who clearly perceives
the fundamental source of a problem
become attached to the factors
that contribute to the complexities
of the world?

64

These factors are transmitted
from one generation to another,
But it is essential to possess a perceptive
and discerning perspective.

65

When examining cause,
consider factors that extend beyond a single cause.
Avoid fixating on the superficial;
instead, direct your attention
towards exploring underlying factors
and depths.

66

I possess four inherent qualities,
and serve as the fundamental source of something.
My labour lacks purpose and is straightforward.
My fate is not determined
by any specific cause.
O unfortunate one!

67

The universe is abundant with solutions,
and every problem remains without remedy
unless your deity reveals a way out.
Though you may presently be unaware,
the truth will become evident when needed.

68

The work produced is a reflection of individual insight.
The ability to perceive consistently prompts decisive
action, leaving no individuals aside from
those in subordinate roles.

69

Actions that are unseen still cause effects,
and these effects are not solely determined
by the initial act.

70

Actions and speech serve
as reflections of your true character
and moral consciousness,
revealing the essence within.

Part 8

What Is
True Wealth?

71

If you search for a precious mineral,
you are considered a jewel yourself.
If you persist in seeking a small piece of bread,
you essentially become nothing but bread.
If you understand this puzzle,
you grasp the concept that what you seek
is what you become.

72

Greed symbolizes the season of autumn,
while satisfaction embodies the season of spring.
There is no delight to be found in the world
during the fall.

73

The joy of poverty is like a wine
that cherishes humility,
for all lovers are captivated by submission,
and modesty is intoxicating.

74

Wealthy people are often impoverished
due to their miserly natures,
while the less fortunate attain riches
through their magnanimity,
or suffer destitution
as a consequence of their greed.

75

Be aware of your limitations,
and avoid reaching excessive heights,
otherwise you may descend
into a state of chaos and conflict.

76

If the sole focus was on material
money and possessions,
I would have generously bestowed
upon you a mouthful of gold.

77

Thoughts are merely manifestations of actions;
dust is simply a representation of wealth.
Words are only expressions of states;
states are nothing more than verbal descriptions.

78

In the journey of existence,
and the multitude of lives
that call upon you
during the act of selflessness,
what significance do riches and
belongings possess?

79

Exert more effort and accumulate wealth,
and maintain a positive attitude,
because all your possessions,
including silver, gold, and riches,
are but the embodiment of evil.

80

When individuals are surrounded
by abundant riches and opulence,
they may develop a sense of superiority,
leading them to isolate themselves
from life around them,
and their own offspring.

Part 9

Ways to
Attain Wealth

81

Apart from the portion destined for eternity,
sustenance does not materialize
through pursuit or exertion.

82

Every living creature,
from the smallest bug to the largest elephant,
is under the divine protection of God,
who is the ultimate provider.

83

Those who practise patience
will be rewarded with sustenance,
while impatience leads
to the exertion of laborious effort.

84

In accordance with faith,
inadequate nourishment stems
from a lack of strong conviction,
as the giver of life
will surely provide sustenance.

85

The Prophet taught that sustenance
is found in remote places and secure entrances.
The keys to overcoming obstacles and unlocking success
lie in our actions, efforts, and achievements.

86

Despite the abundance of wealth
and resources in the world,
a devout follower of God
will only partake in what is permissible.

87

Partake in the knowledge bestowed by God,
as He graciously imparts it
without any hidden agenda.

88

The nourishment bestowed by the divine
is imbued with profound insight,
ensuring that it does not become a source
of hardship in the long run.

89

The journey towards obtaining sustenance
requires exertion and labour;
each individual possesses their own
occupation and pursuit.

90

To achieve abundant nourishment,
embrace virtuous behaviour and character;
in this way your sustenance will multiply significantly,
and blessings will be immeasurable.

Part 10

The Impact of Wealth
on a Person's Character

91

An exquisite fragment
that bestows illumination and flawlessness,
obtained through legitimate means of income.

92

Lawful sustenance yields abundant knowledge and wisdom; these morsels give rise to love and affection.

93

Envy and entrapment arise
when one indulges in prohibited indulgence.
It is crucial to recognize that ignorance
and neglect are also deemed forbidden.

94

Upon tasting a morsel,
a strong inclination to serve
and a steadfast determination
to embark on a journey
to that realm emerge.

95

The morsel serves as a seed
from which thoughts emerge;
the morsel symbolizes a vast sea,
and thoughts are its precious jewels.

96

As you experience darkness and fatigue,
be aware that you have a partner
in the Devil.

97

Is there any variety of wheat
that yields barley or oats?
Have you seen a horse
that eats donkey droppings!

98

Just as oil extinguishes a lamp,
and water drowns its own source.

99

A beggar must avoid consuming food
acquired through oppression,
as well as any prohibited foods,
or those acquired through
prioritizing material possessions.
This is because such food
may corrupt the beggar's thoughts
and beliefs.

100

The essence and pinnacle of excellence are legitimate:
you are not flawless,
nor will you remain silent.

Finis

www.ingramcontent.com/pod-product-compliance
Lightning Source LLC
Chambersburg PA
CBHW020450100426
42813CB00031B/3313/J